Learn 'n' Enjoy

SHAPES

Discovery Kidz

Published By
DISCOVERY PUBLISHING HOUSE PVT. LTD.

**4383/4 - A, ANSARI ROAD, DARYA GANJ,
NEW DELHI - 110002 (INDIA)
TEL : +91-11-23279245 / 43596064 / 43596065
FAX : +91-11-23253475
E-MAIL : parul.wasan@gmail.com
info@discoverykidz.in
WEB :- www.discoverykidz.in**

SHAPE ONE

SQUARE

OBJECT ONE

THIS CARROMBOARD IS A SQUARE

SHAPE TWO

RECTANGLE

OBJECT TWO

THIS BLACKBOARD IS A RECTANGLE

SHAPE THREE

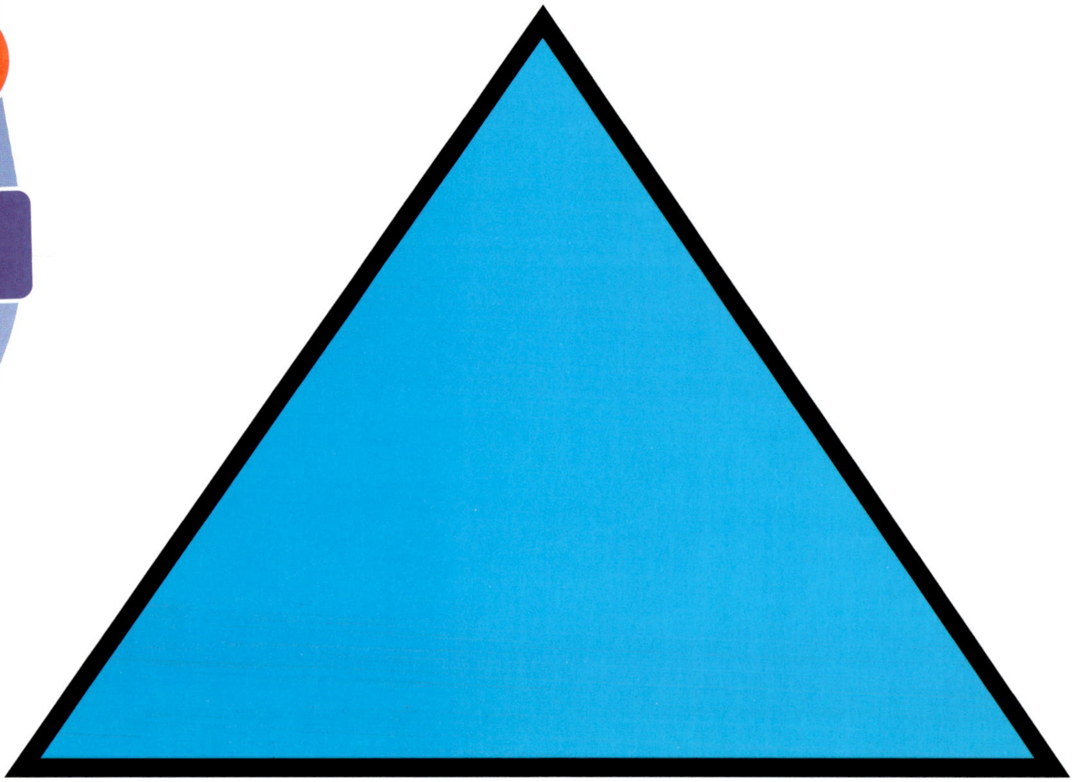

TRIANGLE

OBJECT THREE

THIS CHEESE IS A TRIANGLE

SHAPE FOUR

CIRCLE

OBJECT FOUR

THIS PLATE IS A CIRCLE

SHAPE FIVE

ELLIPSE

OBJECT FIVE

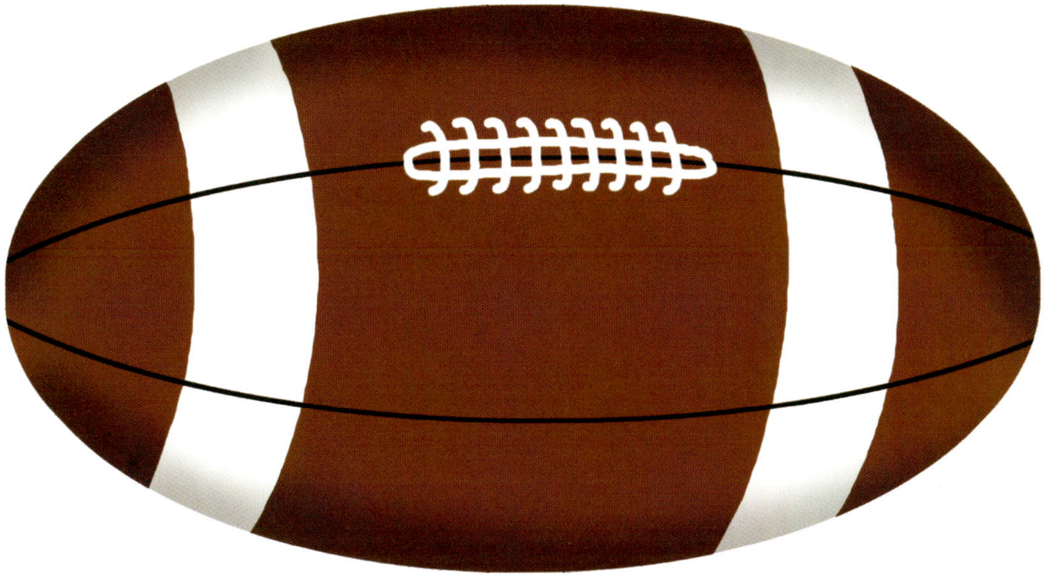

THIS RUGBY BALL IS AN ELLIPSE

SHAPE SIX

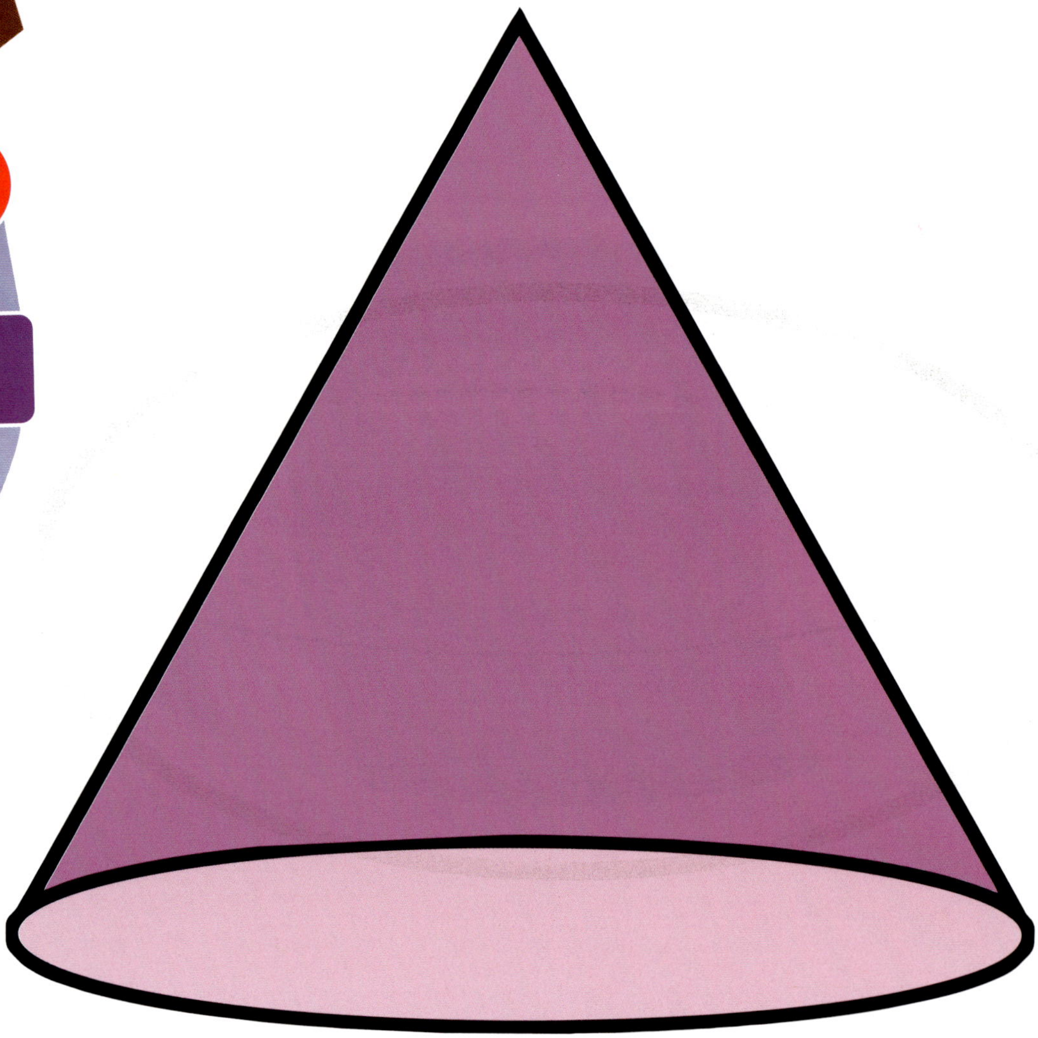

CONE

OBJECT SIX

THIS BIRTHDAY CAP IS A CONE

SHAPE SEVEN

CYLINDER

OBJECT SEVEN

THIS CRACKER IS A CYLINDER

SQUARE

RECTANGLE

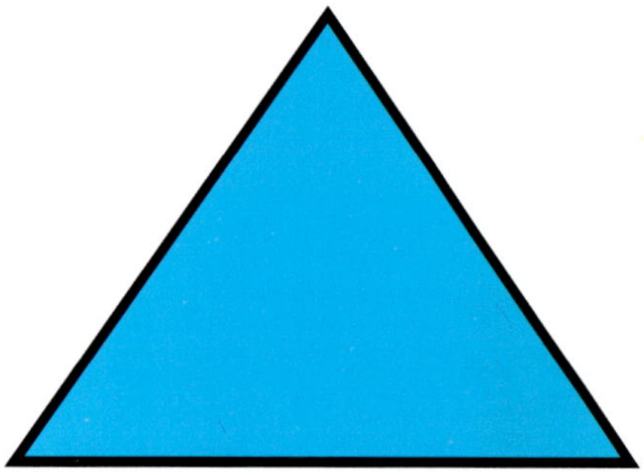

TRIANGLE

CIRCLE

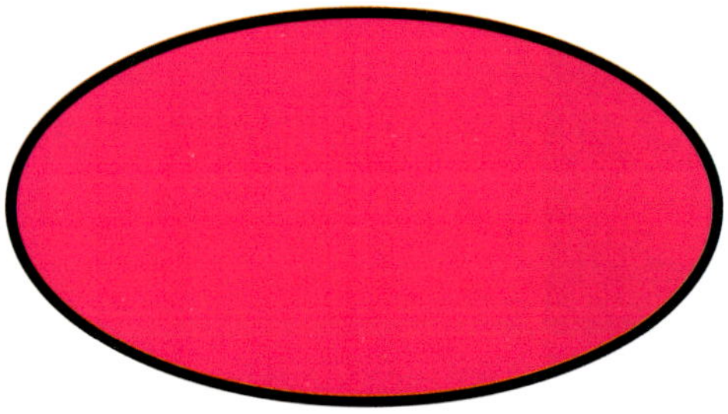

ELLIPSE

CYLINDER

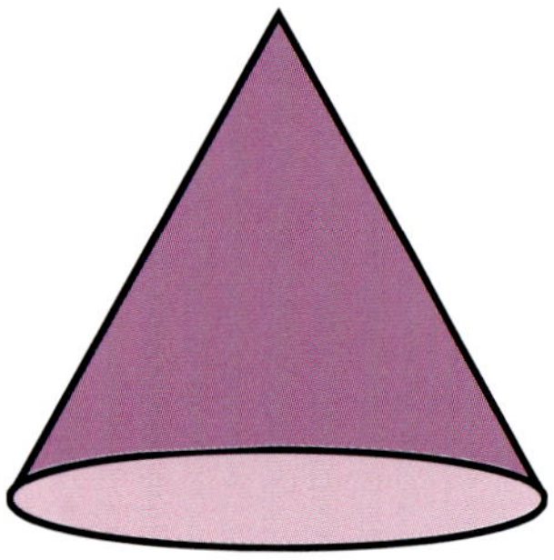

CONE